MADE FROM SC[RAPS]

BISCUIT QUILTS

You will love the puffy softness of these fast, fun and easy to make "biscuit" quilts. The eight patchwork projects – including a baby quilt, lap throws, a wall hanging, and a pillow – are pieced using a variety of fabrics from homespun plaids to cotton prints. The "biscuit" look is achieved by sandwiching extra-loft batting between the backing and a slightly larger top square. Making tiny tucks in the excess fabric, simply sew the squares, with backsides together, clip the exposed seams, then wash to fluff the seams. Follow our clear-cut instructions and your project will be finished in no time – ready to snuggle under or give to a loved one!

LEISURE ARTS, INC.
Little Rock, AR

BISCUITS AROUND THE WORLD

Block Size: 4" x 4" (10.16 cm x 10.16 cm)
Quilt Size: 44" x 60" (111.76 cm x 152.40 cm)

*To make your project easier and more enjoyable, we encourage you to carefully read **The Basics**, page 32, before beginning your project.*

MATERIALS

Yardage is based on 45" (114.3 cm) wide fabric with 42" (106.68 cm) usable width.

$2^1/_8$ yds (1.94 m) **each** of red plaid, red/green plaid, blue plaid, and red/blue plaid for blocks and backings

44" x 60" (111.76 cm x 152.40 cm) piece of extra-loft batting

You will also need:

Water-soluble fabric marking pen
Gridded template plastic

CUTTING INSTRUCTIONS

Note: *Cut all strips across the width of the fabric.*

From red plaid, cut:
- 6 strips, $5^3/_4$"w; subcut into 41 squares, $5^3/_4$" x $5^3/_4$", for Block 1's.
- 6 strips, $5^1/_2$"w; subcut into 41 squares, $5^1/_2$" x $5^1/_2$", for Block 1 backings.

From red/green plaid, cut:
- 6 strips, $5^3/_4$"w; subcut into 40 squares, $5^3/_4$" x $5^3/_4$", for Block 2's.
- 6 strips, $5^1/_2$"w; subcut into 40 squares, $5^1/_2$" x $5^1/_2$", for Block 2 backings.

From *each* of blue and red/blue plaids, cut:
- 6 strips, $5^3/_4$"w; subcut into 42 squares, $5^3/_4$" x $5^3/_4$", for Blocks 3 and 4.
- 6 strips, $5^1/_2$"w; subcut into 42 squares, $5^1/_2$" x $5^1/_2$", for Block 3 and 4 backings.

From extra-loft batting, cut:
- 165 squares, $5^3/_4$" x $5^3/_4$".

ASSEMBLING THE BLOCKS

1. Trace the **Quilting Template**, page 4, onto a piece of gridded template plastic; cut out.
2. Place the template on each corner of the wrong side of each **block backing** and draw a line (**Fig. 1**).
3. Follow **Layering And Quilting The Blocks**, page 28, to layer the backing and batting and quilt on the marked lines (**Fig. 2**).

Fig. 1

Fig. 2

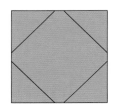
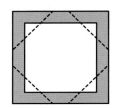

4. Follow **Making A Biscuit**, page 28, to sew the block top to the matching backing and batting. Make 41 of **Block 1**. Make 40 of **Block 2**. Make 42 **each** of **Blocks 3 and 4**.

Block 1 (make 41)

Block 2 (make 40)

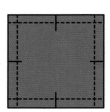
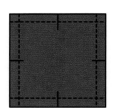

Block 3 (make 42)

Block 4 (make 42)

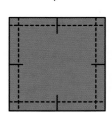
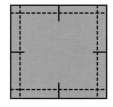

FINISHING

1. Follow **Assembling the Quilt Top**, page 29, to sew the blocks together, referring to the **Quilt Top Diagram**.
2. Topstitch around the outside edge of the quilt on top of the previous row of stitches.
3. Follow **Fringing** and **Washing and Drying**, page 31, to complete the quilt.

Quilting Template

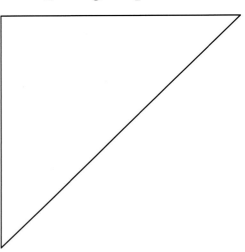

Quilt Top Diagram

1	4	3	2	1	4	1	2	3	4	1
4	3	2	1	4	3	4	1	2	3	4
3	2	1	4	3	2	3	4	1	2	3
2	1	4	3	2	1	2	3	4	1	2
1	4	3	2	1	4	1	2	3	4	1
4	3	2	1	4	3	4	1	2	3	4
3	2	1	4	3	2	3	4	1	2	3
2	1	4	3	2	1	2	3	4	1	2
3	2	1	4	3	2	3	4	1	2	3
4	3	2	1	4	3	4	1	2	3	4
1	4	3	2	1	4	1	2	3	4	1
2	1	4	3	2	1	2	3	4	1	2
3	2	1	4	3	2	3	4	1	2	3
4	3	2	1	4	3	4	1	2	3	4
1	4	3	2	1	4	1	2	3	4	1

BISCUITS FOR BABY

BISCUITS FOR BABY

Block Size: 6" x 6" (15.24 cm x 15.24 cm)
Quilt Size: 30" x 42" (76.20 cm x 106.68 cm)

*To make your project easier and more enjoyable, we encourage you to carefully read **The Basics**, page 32, before beginning your project.*

MATERIALS

Yardage is based on 45" (114.3 cm) wide fabric with 42" (106.68 cm) usable width.

1 yd (0.91 m) of medium-colored fabric for Block 1's
1 yd (0.91 m) of light-colored fabric for Block 2's
1³/₄ yds (1.6 m) of baby flannel for backings

You will also need:

30" x 42" (76.20 cm x 106.68 cm) piece of extra-loft batting
Water-soluble fabric marking pen
Gridded template plastic

CUTTING INSTRUCTIONS

***Note**: Cut all strips across the width of the fabric.*

From medium-colored fabric, cut:
- 4 strips, 7³/₄"w; subcut into 18 squares, 7³/₄" x 7³/₄", for Block 1's.

From light-colored fabric, cut:
- 4 strips, 7³/₄"w; subcut into 17 squares, 7³/₄" x 7³/₄", for Block 2's.

From baby flannel, cut:
- 7 strips, 7¹/₂"w; subcut into 35 squares, 7¹/₂" x 7¹/₂", for backings.

From extra-loft batting, cut:
- 35 squares, 5³/₄" x 5³/₄".

ASSEMBLING THE BLOCKS

1. Mark the center of each of the medium- and light-colored fabric squares on the right side for "dimpling" (**Fig. 1**).

Fig. 1

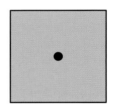

2. Trace the **Quilting Template** onto a piece of gridded template plastic; cut out.
3. Place the template on each corner of the wrong side of each **block backing** and draw a line (**Fig. 2**).

Fig. 2

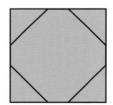

4. Follow **Layering And Quilting The Blocks**, page 28, to layer the backing and batting and quilt on the marked lines (**Fig. 3**).

Fig. 3

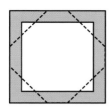

5.   Follow **Making A Biscuit**, page 28, to sew the block top to the backing and batting. Make 18 **Block 1's** and 17 **Block 2's**.

Block 1 (make 18)   **Block 2** (make 17)

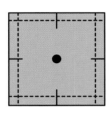   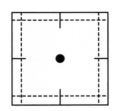

6.   Follow **Adding A Dimple**, page 29, to tack the center of each block.

FINISHING

1.   Follow **Assembling the Quilt Top**, page 29, to sew the blocks together, referring to the **Quilt Top Diagram**.
2.   Topstitch around the outside edge of the quilt on top of the previous row of stitches.
3.   Follow **Fringing** and **Washing and Drying**, page 31, to complete the quilt.

Quilt Top Diagram

1	2	1	2	1
2	1	2	1	2
1	2	1	2	1
2	1	2	1	2
1	2	1	2	1
2	1	2	1	2
1	2	1	2	1

Quilting Template

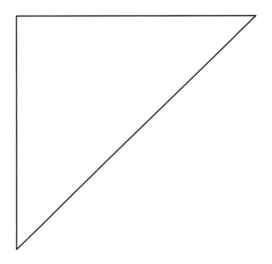

GINGHAM BISCUITS

Block Size: 5¹/₂" x 5¹/₂" (13.97 cm x 13.97 cm)
Quilt Size: 38¹/₂" x 49¹/₂" (97.79 cm x 125.73 cm)

*To make your project easier and more enjoyable, we encourage you to carefully read **The Basics**, page 32, before beginning your project.*

MATERIALS

Yardage is based on 45" (114.3 cm) wide fabric with 42" (106.68 cm) usable width.
   *2¹/₂ yds (2.29 m) of blue lightweight denim
   1³/₈ yds (1.26 m) of osnaburg
   3 yds (2.74 m) of blue/beige plaid
You will also need:
39" x 50" (99.06 cm x 127 cm) piece of extra-loft batting
Water-soluble fabric marking pen
Gridded template plastic

*You will need only 2 yds (1.83 m) if purchasing 60" (152.4 cm) wide denim.

CUTTING INSTRUCTIONS

***Note**: Cut all strips across the width of the fabric.*
From blue lightweight denim, cut:
- 4 strips, 7¹/₄"w (or 3 strips, 7¹/₄" x 60"); subcut into 20 squares, 7¹/₄" x 7¹/₄", for Block 1's.
- 4 strips, 7"w (or 3 strips, 7" x 60"); subcut into 20 squares, 7" x 7", for Block 1 backings.
- 5 strips, 5"w (or 4 strips, 5" x 60"), for binding.

From osnaburg, cut:
- 3 strips, 7¹/₄"w; subcut into 12 squares, 7¹/₄" x 7¹/₄", for Block 2's.
- 2 strips, 7"w; subcut into 12 squares, 7" x 7", for Block 2 backings.

From blue/beige plaid, cut:
- 7 strips, 7¹/₄"w; subcut into 31 squares, 7¹/₄" x 7¹/₄", for Block 3's.
- 6 strips, 7"w; subcut into 31 squares, 7" x 7", for Block 3 backings.

From extra-loft batting, cut:
- 63 squares, 5¹/₄" x 5¹/₄".

ASSEMBLING THE BLOCKS

1. Mark the center of each 7¹/₄" fabric square on the right side for "dimpling" (**Fig. 1**).

Fig. 1

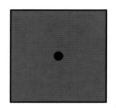

2. Trace the **Quilting Template**, page 10, onto a piece of gridded template plastic; cut out.
3. Place the template on each corner of the wrong side of each **block backing** and draw a line (**Fig. 2**).

Fig. 2

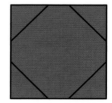

4. Follow **Layering And Quilting The Blocks**, page 28, to layer the backing and batting and quilt on the marked lines (**Fig. 3**).

Fig. 3

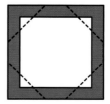

5. Follow **Making A Biscuit**, page 28, to sew the block top to the matching backing and batting. See the diagrams below for the quantity needed of each block.

Block 1 (make 20)

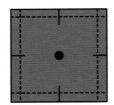

Block 2 (make 12)

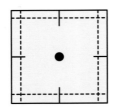

Block 3 (make 31)

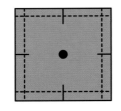

6. Follow **Adding A Dimple**, page 29, to tack the center of each block.

FINISHING

1. Follow **Assembling the Quilt Top**, page 29, to sew the blocks together, referring to the **Quilt Top Diagram**.
2. Follow **Frayed-Edge Binding**, page 30, to add binding to the quilt.
3. Follow **Fringing** and **Washing and Drying**, page 31, to complete the quilt.

Quilt Top Diagram

1	3	1	3	1	3	1
3	2	3	2	3	2	3
1	3	1	3	1	3	1
3	2	3	2	3	2	3
1	3	1	3	1	3	1
3	2	3	2	3	2	3
1	3	1	3	1	3	1
3	2	3	2	3	2	3
1	3	1	3	1	3	1

Quilting Template

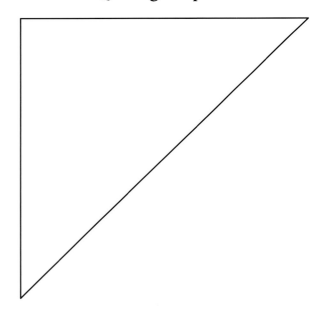

PINWHEELS

PINWHEELS

Block Size: 4¹/₂" x 4¹/₂" (11.43 cm x 11.43 cm)
Quilt Size: 36" x 54" (91.44 cm x 137.16 cm)

*To make your project easier and more enjoyable, we encourage you to carefully read **The Basics**, page 32, before beginning your project.*

MATERIALS
Yardage is based on 45" (114.3 cm) wide fabric with 42" (106.68 cm) usable width.
- 1¹/₈ yds (1.03 m) of blue plaid (**A**)
- 1¹/₈ yds (1.03 m) of blue/white plaid (**B**)
- 1¹/₈ yds (1.03 m) of red plaid (**C**)
- 1¹/₈ yds (1.03 m) of red/white plaid (**D**)
- 3¹/₄ yds (2.97 m) of blue/red plaid (**E**)

You will also need:
- 36" x 54" (91.44 cm x 137.16 cm) piece of extra-loft batting
- Water-soluble fabric marking pen
- Gridded template plastic

CUTTING INSTRUCTIONS
Note: *Cut all strips across the width of the fabric.*
From each plaid (A, B, C, & D), cut:
- 3 strips, 7¹/₈"w; subcut into 15 squares, 7¹/₈" x 7¹/₈", for half-square triangle blocks.
- 2 strips, 6"w; subcut into 12 squares, 6" x 6", for backings.

From blue/red plaid (E), cut:
- 8 strips, 7¹/₈"w; subcut into 36 squares, 7¹/₈" x 7¹/₈", for half-square triangle blocks.
- 7 or 8 strips, 6"w; subcut into 48 squares, 6" x 6", for backings.

From extra-loft batting, cut:
- 96 squares, 4¹/₄" x 4¹/₄"

ASSEMBLING THE BLOCKS

1. Follow **Steps 2 – 10**, page 13, to make 96 blocks using the fabric combinations shown in the diagrams below. Press seams in the direction of the arrows. The backing fabric to be used for each block in Step 9 is shown in parentheses below the block.

Block 1A (make 6)

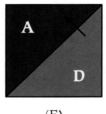

(E)

Block 1B (make 6)

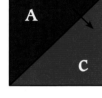

(3-A, 3-C)

Block 1C (make 12)

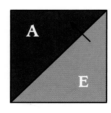

(3-B, 3-D, 6-E)

Block 1D (make 12)

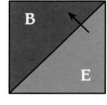

(3-B, 3-D, 6-E)

Block 1E (make 12)

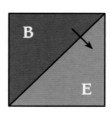

(3-A, 3-C, 6-E)

Block 2A (make 6)

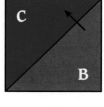

(E)

Block 2B (make 6)

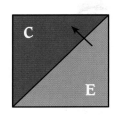

(3-A, 3-C)

Block 2C (make 12)

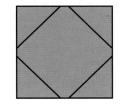

(3-B, 3-D, 6-E)

Block 2D (make 12)

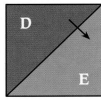

(3-B, 3-D, 6-E)

Block 2E (make 12)

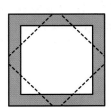

(3-A, 3-C, 6-E)

2. Mark a diagonal line from corner to corner on the wrong side of the 7$\frac{1}{8}$" squares.
3. Pin fabrics right sides together with the grain going in opposite directions and the marked fabric on top (**Fig. 1**).
4. Refer to **Fig. 2** to sew $\frac{1}{4}$" from each side of the marked line.
5. Cut on the marked line to make 2 blocks (**Fig. 3**).
6. Press the seam in each block toward the darker fabric (**Fig. 4**).

Fig. 1

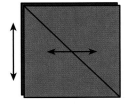

Fig. 2

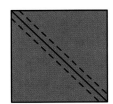

Fig. 3

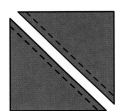

Fig. 4

7. Trace the **Quilting Template**, page 14, onto a piece of gridded template plastic; cut out.
8. Place the template on each corner of the wrong side of each **block backing** and draw a line (**Fig. 5**).
9. Follow **Layering And Quilting The Blocks**, page 28, to layer the backing and batting and quilt on the marked lines (**Fig. 6**).

Fig. 5

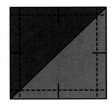

Fig. 6

10. Follow **Making A Biscuit**, page 28, to sew the block top to the backing and batting using the backing fabric shown in parentheses in the diagrams in Step 1. Make 96 blocks (**Fig. 7**).

Fig. 7

FINISHING

1. Follow **Assembling the Quilt Top**, page 29, to sew the blocks together in groups of 16, following the diagrams, page 14, for placement and paying attention to the arrows indicating the direction of pressing. Make 3 of each group.

Group 1 (make 3)

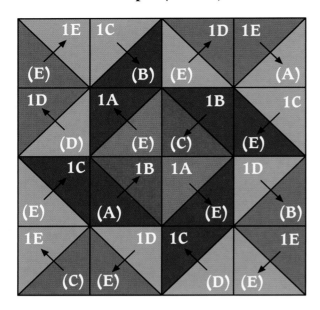

Quilt Top Diagram

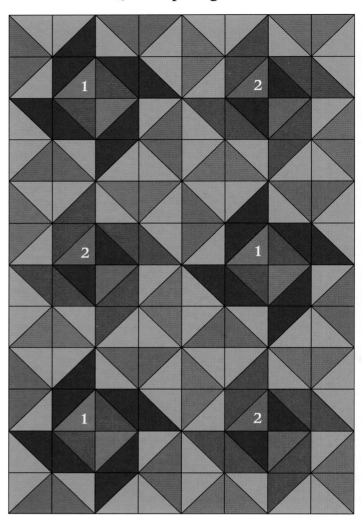

Group 2 (make 3)

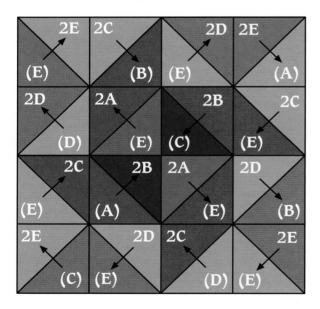

Quilting Template

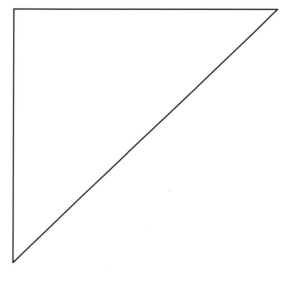

2. Sew the groups together, referring to the **Quilt Top Diagram** and being careful not to rotate the groups.
3. Topstitch around the outside edge of the quilt on top of the previous row of stitches.
4. Follow **Fringing** and **Washing and Drying**, page 31, to complete the quilt.

14

NINE-PATCH TRIO

NINE-PATCH LAP QUILT

Block Size: 5" x 5" (12.70 cm x 12.70 cm)
Quilt Size: 45" x 45" (114.30 cm x 114.30 cm)

*To make your project easier and more enjoyable, we encourage you to carefully read **The Basics**, page 32, before beginning your project.*

MATERIALS

Yardage is based on 45" (114.3 cm) wide fabric with 42" (106.68 cm) usable width.

$1^5/_8$ yds (1.49 m) of lavender/pink plaid (**A**)
$1^7/_8$ yds (1.71 m) of pink plaid (**B**)
$2^5/_8$ yds (2.4 m) of lavender/green plaid (**C**)
$1^1/_2$ yds (1.37 m) of light green plaid (**D**)

You will also need:

45" x 45" (114.30 cm x 114.30 cm) piece of extra-loft batting
Water-soluble fabric marking pen
Gridded template plastic

CUTTING INSTRUCTIONS

Note: *Cut all strips across the width of the fabric.*

From lavender/pink plaid (A), cut:

- 5 strips, $6^3/_4$"w; subcut into 25 squares, $6^3/_4$" x $6^3/_4$", for plain blocks.
- 2 strips, $7^1/_2$"w; subcut into 8 squares, $7^1/_2$" x $7^1/_2$", for hourglass blocks.

From pink plaid (B), cut:

- 4 strips, $6^3/_4$"w; subcut into 24 squares, $6^3/_4$" x $6^3/_4$", for plain blocks.
- 2 strips, $7^1/_2$"w; subcut into 8 squares, $7^1/_2$" x $7^1/_2$", for hourglass blocks.
- 2 strips, $7^1/_8$"w; subcut into 8 squares, $7^1/_8$" x $7^1/_8$", for half-square triangle blocks.

From lavender/green plaid (C), cut:

- 2 strips, $7^1/_8$"w; subcut into 8 squares, $7^1/_8$" x $7^1/_8$", for half-square triangle blocks.
- 7 strips, $6^1/_2$"w; subcut into 40 squares, $6^1/_2$" x $6^1/_2$", for backings.
- 5 strips, 5"w, for binding.

From light green plaid (D), cut:

- 7 strips, $6^1/_2$"w; subcut into 41 squares, $6^1/_2$" x $6^1/_2$", for backings.

From extra-loft batting, cut:

- 81 squares, $4^3/_4$" x $4^3/_4$".

ASSEMBLING THE BLOCKS

1. Follow **Steps 2 - 6**, below, to make 16 **Block 1's** using the pink (B) and lavender/green (C) $7^1/_8$" squares.

Block 1 (make 16)

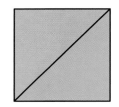

2. Mark a diagonal line from corner to corner on the wrong side of the lighter fabric.
3. Pin fabrics right sides together with the grain going in opposite directions and the marked fabric on top (**Fig. 1**).
4. Refer to **Fig. 2** to sew $1/_4$" from each side of the marked line.

Fig. 1

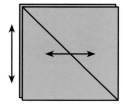

Fig. 2

5. Cut on the marked line to make 2 blocks (**Fig. 3**).
6. Press the seam in each block toward the darker fabric (**Fig. 4**).

Fig. 3 **Fig. 4**

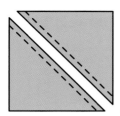 

7. Follow **Steps 8 - 13**, below, to make 16 **Block 2's**.

Block 2 (make 16)

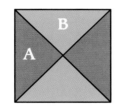

8. Follow **Steps 2 - 6**, above, to make 2 Half-Square Triangles using the lavender/pink (A) and pink (B) $7^1/2$" squares.
9. Mark a diagonal line from corner to corner on the wrong side of one of the Half-Square Triangles (**Fig. 5**).
10. Pin blocks right sides together with the dark and light triangles **opposite** each other and the marked unit on top, carefully matching seams.
11. Sew $^1/4$" from each side of the marked line (**Fig. 6**).

Fig. 5 **Fig. 6**

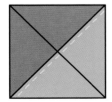 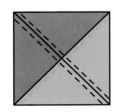

12. Cut on the marked line to make 2 blocks (**Fig. 7**).
13. Press the seams in each block toward the darker fabric and open at the center (**Fig. 8**).

Fig. 7 **Fig. 8**

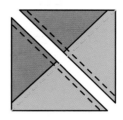 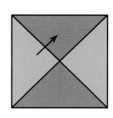

14. Mark the center of each of the $6^3/4$" fabric squares and Block 1's on the right side for "dimpling" (**Fig. 9**).

Fig. 9

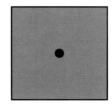 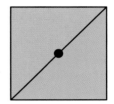

15. Trace the **Quilting Template**, page 18, onto a piece of gridded template plastic; cut out.
16. Place the template on each corner of the wrong side of each **block backing** and draw a line (**Fig. 10**).
17. Follow **Layering And Quilting The Blocks**, page 28, to layer the backing and batting and quilt on the marked lines (**Fig. 11**).

Fig. 10 **Fig. 11**

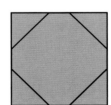 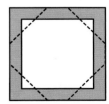

18. Follow **Making A Biscuit**, page 28, to sew the block top to the backing and batting. See the diagrams below for the quantity needed of each block. Use the backing fabric in parentheses.

Block 1 (make 16)

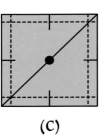

(C)

Block 2 (make 16)

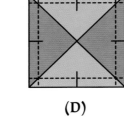

(D)

Block 3 (make 25)

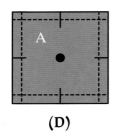

(D)

Block 4 (make 24)

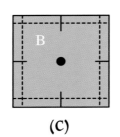

(C)

19. Follow **Adding A Dimple**, page 29, to tack the center of each block.

Quilting Template

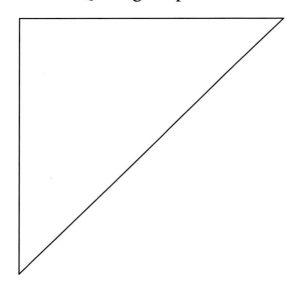

FINISHING

1. Follow **Assembling the Quilt Top**, page 29, to sew the blocks together in groups of 9, following the diagrams below for placement. Make 5 **Group A's** and 4 **Group B's**.

Group A (make 5)

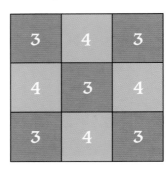

Group B (make 4)

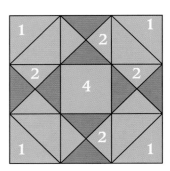

2. Follow **Assembling the Quilt Top** to sew the groups together, referring to the **Quilt Top Diagram**.

3. Follow **Frayed-Edge Binding**, page 30, to add binding to the quilt.

4. Follow **Fringing** and **Washing and Drying**, page 31, to complete the quilt.

Quilt Top Diagram

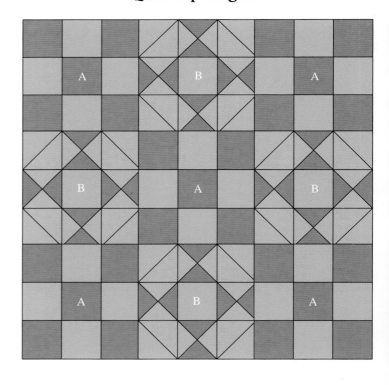

NINE-PATCH WALL QUILT

Center Block Size: 5" x 5" (12.70 cm x 12.70 cm)
Border Block Size: 3" x 3" (7.62 cm x 7.62 cm)
Quilt Size: 21" x 21" (53.34 cm x 53.34 cm)

*To make your project easier and more enjoyable, we encourage you to carefully read **The Basics**, page 32, before beginning your project.*

MATERIALS

Yardage is based on 45" (114.3 cm) wide fabric with 42" (106.68 cm) usable width.

1 yd (0.91 m) of lavender/pink plaid (**A**)
^{1}/4 yd (22.86 cm) of pink plaid (**B**)
^{3}/4 yd (68.58 cm) of lavender/green plaid (**C**)
^{1}/4 yd (22.86 cm) of light green plaid (**D**)

You will also need:

21" x 21" (53.34 cm x 53.34 cm) piece of extra-loft batting
Water-soluble fabric marking pen
Gridded template plastic

CUTTING INSTRUCTIONS

From lavender/pink plaid (A), cut:
- 2 squares, 7^1/2" x 7^1/2", for hourglass blocks.
- 12 squares, 4^3/4" x 4^3/4", for 3" plain blocks.
- 12 squares, 4^1/2" x 4^1/2", for 3" plain blocks backing.
- 1 strip, 4" x 20", for hanging sleeve.

From pink plaid (B), cut:
- 1 square, 7^1/2" x 7^1/2", for hourglass blocks.
- 4 squares, 6^3/4" x 6^3/4", for 5" plain blocks.

From lavender/green plaid (C), cut:
- 1 square, 6^3/4" x 6^3/4", for 5" plain block.
- 5 squares, 6^1/2" x 6^1/2", for 5" plain blocks backing.
- 12 squares, 4^3/4" x 4^3/4", for 3" plain blocks.
- 12 squares, 4^1/2" x 4^1/2", for 3" plain blocks backing.

From light green plaid (D), cut:
- 1 square, 7^1/2" x 7^1/2", for hourglass blocks.
- 4 squares, 6^1/2" x 6^1/2", for hourglass blocks backing.

From extra-loft batting, cut:
- 9 squares, 4^3/4" x 4^3/4".
- 24 squares, 2^3/4" x 2^3/4".

ASSEMBLING THE BLOCKS

1. Follow **Steps 2 - 6**, below, to make 2 Half-Square Triangles using the lavender/pink and pink plaid 7^1/2" squares. Repeat to make 2 Half-Square Triangles using the lavender/pink and light green plaid 7^1/2" squares.
2. Mark a diagonal line from corner to corner on the wrong side of the lighter fabric.
3. Pin fabrics right sides together with the grain going in opposite directions and the marked fabric on top (**Fig. 1**).
4. Refer to **Fig. 2** to sew ^{1}/4" from each side of the marked line.
5. Cut on the marked line to make 2 blocks (**Fig. 3**).
6. Press the seam in each block toward the darker fabric (**Fig. 4**).

Fig. 1

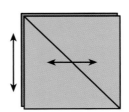

Fig. 2

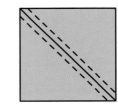

Fig. 3

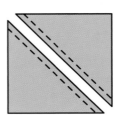

Fig. 4

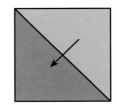

7. Mark a diagonal line from corner to corner on the wrong side of 1 of the Half-Square Triangle Blocks (**Fig. 5**). With right sides together, place the Blocks together with the dark and light triangles **opposite** each other and the marked unit on top, carefully matching seams. Sew ¹/₄" from each side on the diagonal line (**Fig. 6**). Cut on the diagonal line to make 2 Blocks (**Fig. 7**). Press the seams in each block toward the darker fabric and open at center (**Fig. 8**).

Fig. 5   **Fig. 6**

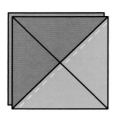   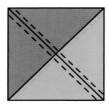

Fig. 7   **Fig. 8** (make 4)

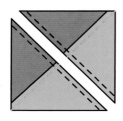   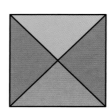

8. Mark the center of each of the pink plaid and lavender/green plain block fabric squares on the right side for "dimpling" (**Fig. 9**).

Fig. 9

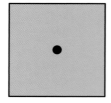

9. Trace the **3"** and **5" Quilting Templates** onto a piece of gridded template plastic; cut out.

10. Place the small template on each corner of the wrong side of each lavender/green plaid **small block backings** and the large template on each corner of the wrong side of each **large block backings** and draw a line (**Fig. 10**).

Fig. 10

11. Follow **Layering And Quilting The Blocks**, page 28, to layer the backing and batting and quilt on the marked lines (**Fig. 11**).

Fig. 11

   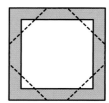

12. Follow **Making A Biscuit**, page 28, to sew the block top to the backing and batting. See the diagrams below for the quantity needed of each block. Use the backing fabric in parentheses.

Block 1 (make 4)   **Block 2** (make 1)

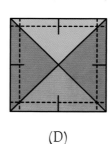   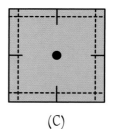

(D)   (C)

Block 3 (make 4)   **Block 4** (make 12)

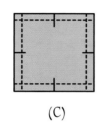

(C)

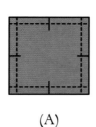

(A)

Block 5 (make 12)

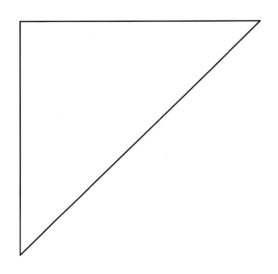

(C)

13. Follow **Adding A Dimple**, page 29, to tack the center of each 5" block.

FINISHING

1. Follow **Assembling the Quilt Top**, page 29, to sew the blocks together, referring to the **Quilt Top Diagram**.
2. If desired, follow **Adding A Hanging Sleeve**, page 31.

3. Topstitch around the outside edge of the quilt on top of the previous row of stitches.
4. Follow **Fringing** and **Washing and Drying**, page 31, to complete the quilt.

Quilt Top Diagram

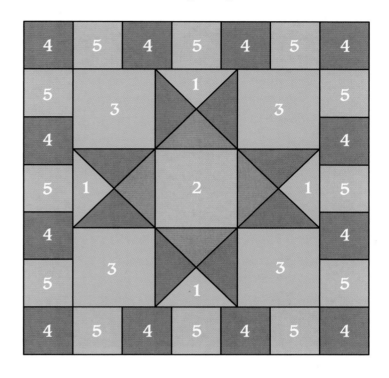

3" Quilting Template

5" Quilting Template

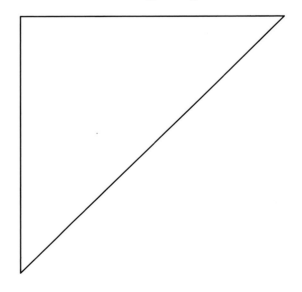

NINE-PATCH PILLOW

Block Size: 4³/₄" x 4³/₄" (12.07 cm x 12.07 cm)
Pillow Size: 14" x 14" (35.56 cm x 35.56 cm)

*To make your project easier and more enjoyable, we encourage you to carefully read **The Basics**, page 32, before beginning your project.*

MATERIALS

Yardage is based on 45" (114.3 cm) wide fabric with 42" (106.68 cm) usable width.
- ¹/₄ yd (22.86 cm) of lavender/pink plaid (**A**)
- ¹/₄ yd (22.86 cm) of pink plaid (**B**)
- ⁵/₈ yd (57.15 cm) of lavender/green plaid (**C**)
- ¹/₄ yd (22.86 cm) of light green plaid (**D**)

You will also need:
- 14" x 14" (35.56 cm x 35.56 cm) piece of extra-loft batting
- 14" (35.56 cm) pillow form
- Water-soluble fabric marking pen
- Gridded template plastic

CUTTING INSTRUCTIONS

From lavender/pink plaid (A), cut:
- 1 square, 6¹/₂" x 6¹/₂", for plain block.
- 2 squares, 6⁷/₈" x 6⁷/₈", for half-square triangle blocks (corners).
- 1 square, 7¹/₄" x 7¹/₄", for combination blocks.

From pink plaid (B), cut:
- 2 squares, 6⁷/₈" x 6⁷/₈", for half-square triangle blocks (corners).
- 1 square, 7¹/₄" x 7¹/₄", for combination blocks.

From lavender/green plaid (C), cut:
- 2 squares, 6⁷/₈" x 6⁷/₈", for combination blocks.
- 4 squares, 6¹/₄" x 6¹/₄", for combination blocks backing.
- 2 rectangles, 10¹/₄" x 15³/₄", for pillow back.

From light green plaid (D), cut:
- 5 squares, 6¹/₄" x 6¹/₄", for Block 1 and plain blocks backing.

From extra-loft batting, cut:
- 9 squares, 4¹/₂" x 4¹/₂".

ASSEMBLING THE BLOCKS

1. Follow **Steps 2 - 6**, below, to make 4 Half-Square Triangles using the lavender/pink and pink plaid 6⁷/₈" squares. These will be used for the 4 corners of the pillow top.
2. Mark a diagonal line from corner to corner on the wrong side of the lighter fabric.
3. Pin fabrics right sides together with the grain going in opposite directions and the marked fabric on top (**Fig. 1**).
4. Refer to **Fig. 2** to sew ¹/₄" from each side of the marked line.
5. Cut on the marked line to make 2 blocks (**Fig. 3**).
6. Press the seam in each block toward the darker fabric (**Fig. 4**).

Fig. 1

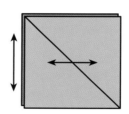

Fig. 2

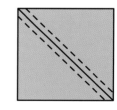

Fig. 3

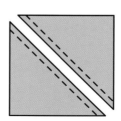

Fig. 4

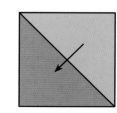

7. Set Block 1's aside.

8. Follow **Steps 9 – 12**, below, to make 4 Combination Blocks, 2 right hand and 2 left hand.
9. Repeat **Steps 2 – 6**, page 22, to make 2 Half-Square Triangles using the lavender/pink and pink plaid 7¹/₄" squares.
10. Mark a diagonal line from corner to corner on the **wrong** side of both of the blocks (**Fig. 5**).
11. With right sides together, place the marked blocks on top of fabric C 6⁷/₈" blocks. Sew ¹/₄" from each side of the marked line (**Fig. 6**).
12. Cut on the marked line on each of the blocks (**Fig. 7**) to make 4 blocks, 2 of each color combination. Press the seam in each block toward fabric C (**Fig. 8**).

Fig. 5   **Fig. 6**

   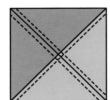

Fig. 7

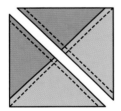

Block 2 (make 2)   **Block 3** (make 2)

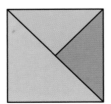

13. Mark the center of each of the squares for plain blocks and Block 1's on the right side for "dimpling" (**Fig. 8**).

Fig. 8

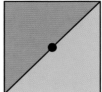

14. Trace the **Quilting Template**, page 24, onto a piece of gridded template plastic; cut out.
15. Place the template on each corner of the wrong side of each **block backing** and draw a line (**Fig. 9**).

Fig. 9

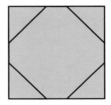

16. Follow **Layering And Quilting The Blocks**, page 28, to layer the backing and batting and quilt on the marked lines (**Fig. 10**).

Fig. 10

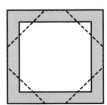

17. Follow **Making A Biscuit**, page 28, to sew the block top to the backing and batting. See the diagrams below for the quantity needed of each block. Use the backing fabric in parenthesis.

Pillow Top Diagram

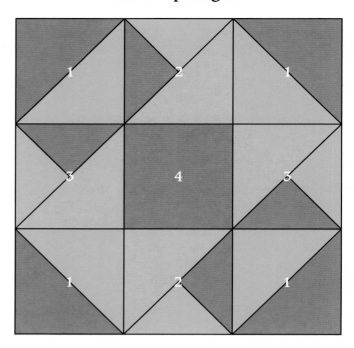

Block 1 (make 4)

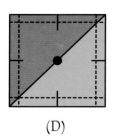

(D)

Block 2 (make 2)

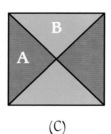

(C)

Block 3 (make 2)

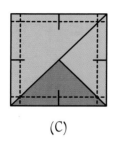

(C)

Block 4 (make 1)

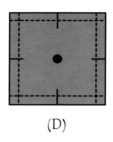

(D)

18. Follow **Adding A Dimple**, page 29, to tack the center of each block.

FINISHING

1. Follow **Assembling the Quilt Top**, page 29, to sew the blocks together, referring to the **Pillow Top Diagram**.
2. Follow **Making A Pillow**, page 31, to finish the pillow.

Quilting Template

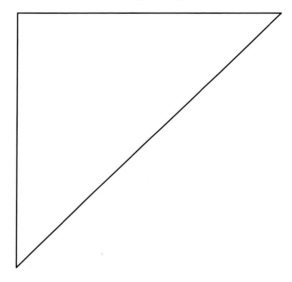

SIMPLY PLAID

SIMPLY PLAID

Block Size: 4$\frac{1}{2}$" x 4$\frac{1}{2}$" (11.43 cm x 11.43 cm)
Quilt Size: 40$\frac{1}{2}$" x 58$\frac{1}{2}$" (102.87 cm x 148.59 cm)

*To make your project easier and more enjoyable, we encourage you to carefully read **The Basics**, page 32, before beginning your project.*

MATERIALS
Yardage is based on 45" (114.3 cm) wide fabric with 42" (106.68 cm) usable width.
$\frac{7}{8}$ yd (80.01 cm) of green fabric (**A**)
$\frac{1}{2}$ yd (45.72 cm) of red fabric (**B**)
1$\frac{5}{8}$ yds (1.49 m) of beige plaid (**C**)
2$\frac{1}{4}$ yds (2.06 m) of green/beige plaid (**D**)
1$\frac{5}{8}$ yds (1.49 m) of red/beige plaid (**E**)
1$\frac{1}{4}$ yds (1.14 m) of red/green plaid (**F**)
You will also need:
41" x 59" (104.14 cm x 149.86 cm) piece of extra-loft batting
Water-soluble fabric marking pen
Gridded template plastic

CUTTING INSTRUCTIONS
Note: *Cut all strips across the width of the fabric.*
From green fabric (A), cut:
- 2 strips, 6$\frac{1}{4}$"w; subcut into 12 squares, 6$\frac{1}{4}$" x 6$\frac{1}{4}$", for Block 1's.
- 2 strips, 6"w; subcut into 12 squares, 6" x 6", for Block 1 backings.

From red fabric (B), cut:
- 1 strip, 6$\frac{1}{4}$"w; subcut into 6 squares, 6$\frac{1}{4}$" x 6$\frac{1}{4}$", for Block 2's.
- 1 strip, 6"w; subcut into 6 squares, 6" x 6", for Block 2 backings.

From beige plaid (C), cut:
- 4 strips, 6$\frac{1}{4}$"w; subcut into 24 squares, 6$\frac{1}{4}$" x 6$\frac{1}{4}$", for Block 3's.
- 4 strips, 6"w; subcut into 24 squares, 6" x 6", for Block 3 backings.

From green/beige plaid (D), cut:
- 6 strips, 6$\frac{1}{4}$"w; subcut into 34 squares, 6$\frac{1}{4}$" x 6$\frac{1}{4}$", for Block 4's.
- 5 strips, 6"w; subcut into 34 squares, 6" x 6", for Block 4 backings.

From red/beige plaid (E), cut:
- 4 strips, 6$\frac{1}{4}$"w; subcut into 24 squares, 6$\frac{1}{4}$" x 6$\frac{1}{4}$", for Block 5's.
- 4 strips, 6"w; subcut into 24 squares, 6" x 6", for Block 5 backings.

From red/green plaid (F), cut:
- 3 strips, 6$\frac{1}{4}$"w; subcut into 17 squares, 6$\frac{1}{4}$" x 6$\frac{1}{4}$", for Block 6's.
- 3 strips, 6"w; subcut into 17 squares, 6" x 6", for Block 6 backings.

From extra-loft batting, cut:
- 117 squares, 4$\frac{1}{4}$" x 4$\frac{1}{4}$".

ASSEMBLING THE BLOCKS
1. Trace the **Quilting Template** onto a piece of gridded template plastic; cut out.
2. Place the template on each corner of the wrong side of each **block backing** and draw a line (**Fig. 1**).
3. Follow **Layering And Quilting The Blocks**, page 28, to layer the backing and batting and quilt on the marked lines (**Fig. 2**).

Fig. 1

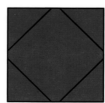

Fig. 2

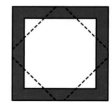

4. Follow **Making A Biscuit**, page 28, to sew the block top to the matching backing and batting. See the diagrams below for the quantity needed of each block.

Block 1 (make 12)

Block 2 (make 6)

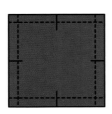

Block 3 (make 24)

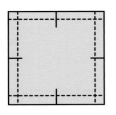

Block 4 (make 34)

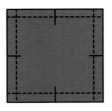

Block 5 (make 24)

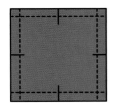

Block 6 (make 17)

FINISHING

1. Follow **Assembling the Quilt Top**, page 29, to sew the blocks together, referring to the **Quilt Top Diagram**.
2. Topstitch around the outside edge of the quilt on top of the previous row of stitches.
3. Follow **Fringing** and **Washing and Drying**, page 31, to complete the quilt.

Quilt Top Diagram

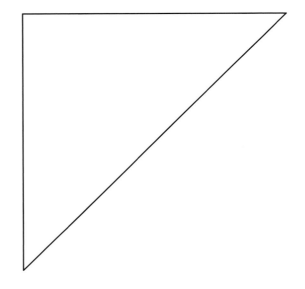

Quilting Template

FRAYED-EDGE BISCUIT TECHNIQUES

The only quilting required for these quilts is to stitch a diagonal line across each corner of the block through the batting and backing only. Blocks larger than 4¹/₂" should be tacked to create a "dimple" at the center after sewing the block top to the backing and batting.

LAYERING AND QUILTING THE BLOCKS

1. Set sewing machine stitch length for 10-12 stitches per inch. Use thread to match or blend with the backing fabrics.
2. Center a batting square on the wrong side of a backing square. Quilt on the marked lines (**Fig. 1**). The batting will cover part of the marked line. Sew straight across the batting, keeping the needle lined up with the marked line on the other side. Complete all 4 sides of one block without cutting the threads before starting the next block.
3. On 3" blocks where the lines overlap, start stitching at the edge of the fabric. Stitch to the point where the lines overlap, turn and stitch down the next side; repeat around, ending at the edge of the fabric (**Fig. 2**).

Fig. 1   **Fig. 2**

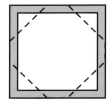   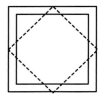

4. Quilting ("dimpling") on larger blocks will be done after block assembly.

ASSEMBLY INSTRUCTIONS

MAKING A BISCUIT

When working the following steps, you may find it easier to chain piece many biscuits at a time rather than trying to make them one at a time.

1. Set sewing machine stitch length for 10-12 stitches per inch. Use matching thread whenever possible and a ⁵/₈" **seam allowance**.

2. Lay a block (top) square on top of a quilted backing and batting square, **wrong** sides together, with the top and right sides of the square even (**Fig. 3**).
3. Begin sewing a ⁵/₈" **seam allowance** along the right edge as shown in **Fig. 4**.

Fig. 3   **Fig. 4**

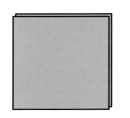   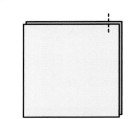

4. Stop sewing after a few stitches and match squares along the bottom and right edges. Make a tuck in the middle of the top square to take up the extra fabric (**Fig. 5**).
5. Continue stitching to the bottom edge of the square.
6. Repeat for the next top and backing square by chain piecing until all squares are sewn on one side (**Fig. 6**). Cut apart.

Fig. 5   **Fig. 6**

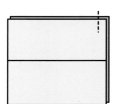   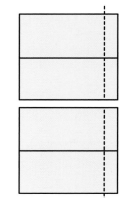

7. Repeat on the remaining three sides. On the final side, the bottom edges will already be lined up.

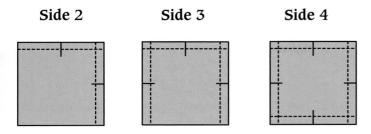

Side 2   Side 3   Side 4

ADDING A DIMPLE

If your finished blocks are more than 4¹/₂" square, the center of each block should be tacked to keep the batting from shifting during washing. The stitches should cover enough threads of the fabric to keep from pulling out during washing.

1. Use a narrow zigzag (about ¹/₈") and a very short stitch. Loosely woven fabrics may require a slightly wider stitch.

2. Slide the finished block under the presser foot and center the needle on the mark at the center of the block.

3. Sew about 12 to 15 stitches followed by a lock stitch. If your sewing machine doesn't have a lock stitch, change to a straight stitch, drop the feed dogs, and sew a half dozen stitches in the same spot.

ASSEMBLING THE QUILT TOP

1. Set sewing machine stitch length for approximately 12-15 stitches per inch. Use a ³/₄" **seam allowance**.

2. Pin blocks with **backing sides together** and sew seams. You will be sewing on the top side of the block (**Fig. 7**).

Fig. 7

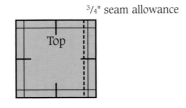

³/₄" seam allowance

Top

3. Lay blocks out to form the quilt top. Sew into horizontal rows, sewing every other row in opposite directions (**Fig. 8**). Press seams open using the tip or edge of the iron to avoid pressing wrinkles into the quilt block.

Fig. 8

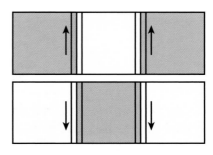

4. Sew rows together to finish the quilt top, alternating directions and carefully matching seams (**Fig. 9**). Press remaining seams **open**.

Fig. 9

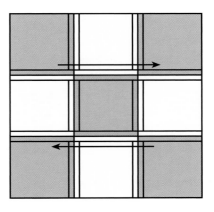

5. To avoid bulk where multiple seams intersect, diagonally trim some of the excess fabric from the underneath seam allowance, as shown by the dotted line (**Fig. 10**).

Fig. 10

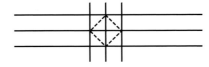

FINISHING INSTRUCTIONS

To finish the quilt, you may either topstitch around the outside edge or apply a frayed-edge binding. Fringing, washing, and drying the quilt will make the exposed seam allowances fuzzy and worn-looking.

FRAYED-EDGE BINDING

1. Piece the binding strips diagonally (**Fig. 11**). Trim excess fabric and press seams open to make one long strip.

Fig. 11

Stitch diagonally.　　　　Trim seam to ¹/₄".　　　　Press seams open.

2. Fold the strip in half lengthwise, wrong sides together, and press.
3. Trim ¹/₄" from the outside edges of the quilt to leave a ¹/₂" seam allowance.
4. Starting near the middle of the top of the quilt on the **back side**, align the **folded edge** of the binding with the **raw edges** of the quilt. Lay binding around quilt to make sure that seams in binding will not end up at a corner. Adjust placement if necessary. Using a walking foot and a **¹/₂" seam allowance**, begin stitching the binding to the quilt, starting 10" from the beginning end of the binding. Stop stitching ¹/₂" from the corner of the quilt; pivot and stitch to the outside corner (**Fig. 12**).

Fig. 12

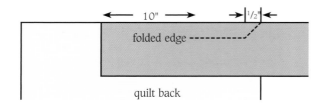

5. Remove the quilt from the machine, and turn the quilt so you will be stitching down the next side. Fold the binding up, away from the quilt, then fold back down in line with the next edge, leaving the top fold even with the raw edge of the previously sewn side (**Fig. 13**). Begin stitching at the top edge, sewing through all layers. Repeat for the remaining edges and corners of the quilt.

Fig. 13

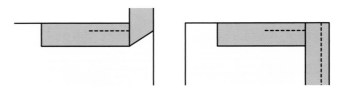

6. On the last side of the quilt, stop stitching about 16" from where you began. Lay both loose ends of the binding flat along the quilt edge (**Fig. 14**). Trim the binding end so the overlap is 5" (**Fig. 15**). Open the two ends of the folded binding, pin wrong sides together at right angles and sew together with a diagonal seam (**Fig. 16**). Trim excess fabric, press seam open, and refold the binding. Align the folded edge with the raw edge of the quilt (**Fig. 17**) and finish sewing it in place.

Fig. 14　　　　　　　**Fig. 15**

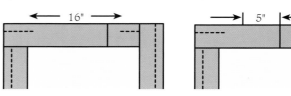

Fig. 16　　　　　　　**Fig. 17**

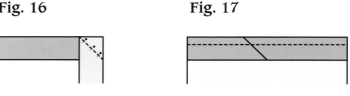

7. Press binding away from the quilt back. Fold the binding to the front of the quilt and pin in place, mitering the corners (**Fig. 18**).

Fig. 18

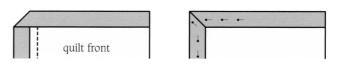

8. Turn the quilt over to the back side and stitch "in the ditch" next to the binding (**Fig. 19**). Remove pins before you get to them. Turn quilt to front side and clip the excess fabric ¹/₄" to ³/₈" apart to fringe the seam (**Fig. 20**). The seam will automatically fold toward the edge of the quilt after washing and drying.

Fig. 19   **Fig. 20**

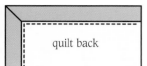   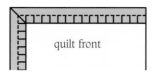

FRINGING
All exposed seam allowances need to be clipped. Start clipping with the last seams sewn and work toward the first seams sewn.

1. Clipping up to but not through the stitching line and cutting no more than two layers of fabric at a time, clip the seam allowances on each seam and the edges of the quilt ¹/₄" to ³/₈" apart.
2. Where the seam allowances are held down by stitching, clip ¹/₈" from the seamline.
3. Clip corners as shown in **Fig. 21**.

Fig. 21

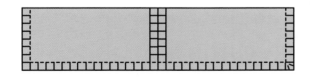

WASHING AND DRYING
You may need to wash and dry your quilt more than once to get the desired results.

1. Shake the quilt outdoors before placing in the washer.
2. If possible, use a washer with a lint trap. Wash quilt using cool water and a short wash cycle.
3. Shake the quilt outdoors again before placing in the dryer.
4. Dry quilt in the dryer on a medium setting. Periodically check the dryer for lint during the cycle.

5. Shake the quilt outdoors again after removing from the dryer.
6. Trim excess fabric at corners if needed. Use the sticky side of masking tape to remove any remaining threads.

OPTIONAL TECHNIQUES
ADDING A HANGING SLEEVE
You may add a hanging sleeve to your project prior to finishing the edges of the quilt.

1. Cut a strip of fabric 2" shorter than the width of the quilt top and 8" wide; piece if necessary.
2. Press short edges ¹/₄" to wrong side; press to wrong side again. Topstitch along folded edges.
3. Fold sleeve in half lengthwise, right sides out, and press.
4. Baste raw edges of sleeve to center back of quilt top, placing it ¹/₄" from the top edge.
5. Topstitch or add frayed-edge binding to edges, treating the hanging sleeve as part of the backing.
6. Hand stitch the folded edge to the back of the quilt.

MAKING A PILLOW
All of the block patterns used for these quilts will work for pillows. (For example: Nine 4" blocks or four 6" blocks will make a 12" pillow.)

1. Follow **Assembling the Quilt Top**, page 29, to sew the blocks together to form the pillow top.
2. Measure the pillow top. For the pillow back, cut 2 rectangles the length of the pillow top and 4" less than the width of the pillow top. (For example: For a 13" square pillow top, the cut size of the pillow backs would be 9" x 13".)
3. Press one long side of each pillow back ³/₈" to wrong side; press to wrong side again. Topstitch along folded edge.
4. Overlapping hemmed edges and aligning raw edges, place the pillow top and pillow backs together, wrong sides facing. (If the hemmed edge falls on a seam, trim a small amount off the unhemmed edge.) Pin in place and sew with a ⁵/₈" seam following the stitching lines on the blocks.
5. Follow **Fringing** and **Washing and Drying**, to fringe, wash, and dry pillow.
6. Insert pillow form.

THE BASICS

*Complete instructions are given for making each of the quilts and the pillow shown in this leaflet. To make your quilting easier and more enjoyable, we encourage you to carefully read all of **Frayed-Edge Biscuit Techniques**, page 28, and these **Basics** and to familiarize yourself with the individual project instructions before beginning a project.*

BASIC TOOLS AND SUPPLIES

CUTTING TOOLS
Rotary Cutter with Extra Blades
Rotary Cutting Mat
Rotary Cutting Rulers – A variety of sizes are available. You may find the following sizes helpful.
- 6" x 24" rectangle – for cutting strips across the fabric width
- 6" square – for subcutting strips, trimming pieced triangle-squares
- 12$^1/_2$" square – for cutting strips or squares larger than 6", squaring fabrics or blocks
- 3" x 18" rectangle – for cutting squares into triangles, cutting narrow strips, marking diagonal lines for quilting

SEWING SUPPLIES
Sewing Machine
- needs a good, even straight stitch and an adjustable needle position or a presser foot that will make an exact $^1/_4$" seam
- helpful to have a lock stitch and needle up or down button

Size 14 Machine Needles
Walking Foot (optional)– helpful when sewing diagonal seams on pieced blocks or adding frayed-edge binding
Quilter's Pins
Cotton-covered Polyester Thread
Scissors
Seam Ripper
Iron and Ironing Surface

OTHER SUPPLIES
Gridded Template Plastic
Marking Pencils
Small Removable Labels (optional) – helpful for labeling blocks or rows to keep them in order
Fine-tip Permanent Fabric Marker

FABRICS AND BATTING

CHOOSING FABRICS
The best fabric choices for these quilts are high-quality 100% cotton homespun plaids or some lightweight flannels. Osnaburg and lightweight denims will also work. Soft cotton prints may be used for the quilt top with homespun or flannel backing.

The yardage requirements given for each project are based on 45" wide fabric with a "usable" width of 42" after shrinkage and trimming selvages. Our recommended yardage lengths should be adequate for occasional resquaring of fabric when many cuts are required.

All fabric should be washed in warm water, dried, and pressed before cutting.

CHOOSING BATTING
Extra-loft batting was used for all of the projects in this leaflet. The batting should be between $^3/_8$" and $^3/_4$" thick for best results.

ROTARY CUTTING

One of the most important steps in making a quilt is cutting the pieces accurately. Plaid fabrics are more challenging to cut, especially if you want to keep the lines in the plaid straight with the seam. By following the instructions below, you should be able to cut the pieces within $^1/_8$" of the straight line of the plaid most of the time. For more perfect cuts, you may prefer cutting them one at a time. The blocks for frayed-edge biscuit quilts are normally larger than those for traditional quilts, so there are not as many pieces to cut.

CUTTING PLAID STRIPS
1. Using scissors, trim one end of the fabric straight with the plaid. Remove the selvage edges (**Fig. 1**).

Fig. 1

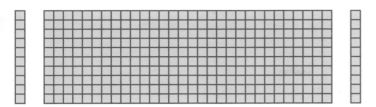

2. Refold the fabric lengthwise (as it was on the bolt) with wrong sides together. Since most homespun plaids do not have a right or wrong side, use the side of your choice.

3. All strips are cut from the selvage-to-selvage width of the fabric unless otherwise instructed. Place fabric on the cutting mat with the fold of the fabric toward you and the trimmed end on the left. Keeping the trimmed edges even, match the plaids at the selvage edge by staggering the selvage edges slightly (**Fig. 2**). Straighten the fabric if necessary by pulling on opposite diagonal corners.

Fig. 2

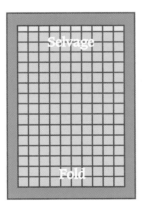

4. Fold the fabric again by bringing the folded edge up to the selvage edge, matching the plaids and keeping trimmed edges even (**Fig. 3**). The folded edge does not have to be perfectly parallel with the selvage edge. It's more important to keep the plaids matched. There will be four layers of fabric. You are now ready to cut the strips.

Fig. 3

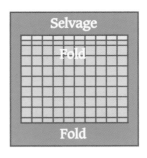

5. Place the ruler over the trimmed edge of the fabric, aligning desired marking on the ruler with the trimmed edge (**Fig. 4**). Check to make sure the right edge of the ruler is lined up as close as possible with a straight line of the plaid. Retract the blade guard on the rotary cutter, and using a smooth downward motion, make the cut by holding the ruler firmly with your left hand and running the blade of the rotary cutter firmly along the right edge of the ruler. Always cut in a direction away from your body and immediately close the blade guard after each cut. If you're cutting multiple strips from the same fabric, you may need to retrim the end of the fabric after several cuts to keep the plaid straight.

Fig. 4

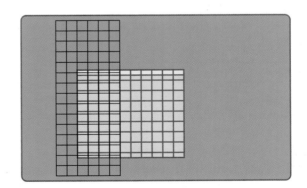

SUBCUTTING PLAID STRIPS

1. Unfold the strips and lay them across the cutting surface, right side up. For faster cutting, layer up to 4 strips by lining up the selvage edges and staggering the strips slightly to line up the plaid. Using the rotary cutter, trim a small amount off the left end of the strips following the straight line of the plaid (**Fig. 5**).

Fig. 5

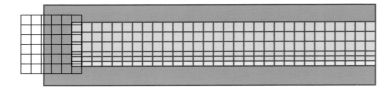

2. To cut squares or rectangles from the strips, place ruler over left end of strips, aligning desired marking on ruler with cut end of strips. If the width is more than the size of the ruler, use the marks on the cutting mat as a guide. Cut on the straight line of the plaid (**Fig. 6**). It's okay if the blocks aren't perfectly square. They can be stretched from corner to corner to square them up. Slight imperfections will be hidden in the fringed seams.

Fig. 6

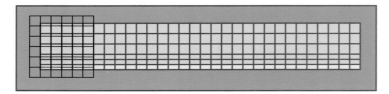

CUTTING SOLIDS OR PRINTS

1. When working with solids or prints, fold the fabric selvage to selvage and align the selvage and folded edge as close as possible with the marks on the cutting mat. Trim the uneven edge square with the folded edge (**Fig. 7**). Fold the fabric again, keeping trimmed edges even, then cut the strips (**Fig. 8**). When cutting multiple strips from the same fabric, make sure the cuts remain at a perfect right angle to the fold. Retrim the uneven edge as needed.

Fig. 7   **Fig. 8**

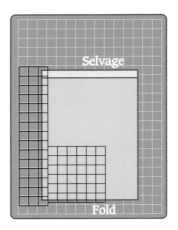
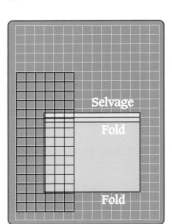

2. Subcut the strips the same as the plaid fabrics. You don't need to stagger the strips. Trim off the selvage edges square with the strip, or cut the first piece slightly larger than needed, rotate the piece and trim to the size needed. For perfectly square cuts, align a horizontal marking on the ruler with one long edge of the strip before cutting (**Fig. 9**).

Fig. 9

CUTTING BATTING
Cutting sizes for batting are given with each individual project.

1. Use a rotary cutter to cut the large batting piece into manageable pieces about the size of your cutting mat.
2. To cut smaller pieces, place one or two layers of batting on cutting mat. Rotary cut all of the strips in one direction, then rotate the mat 90° and rotary cut all of the strips in the other direction.

PIECING AND PRESSING
Precise cutting, followed by accurate piecing and careful pressing, will ensure that all the pieces of your quilt fit together well.

PIECING

- Set sewing machine stitch length for approximately 12-15 stitches per inch (2.0 on some machines).
- Use a new, sharp needle suited for medium-weight woven fabric.
- Use a neutral-colored general-purpose sewing thread (not quilting thread) in the needle and in the bobbin.
- Stitch first on a scrap of fabric to check upper and bobbin thread tension; make any adjustments necessary.
- A variety of seam allowances is used in making these quilts. Check the instructions for the correct size seam allowance.

Chain Piecing

1. Stack the pieces you will be sewing beside your machine in the order you will need them and in a position that will allow you to easily pick them up.
2. Pick up each pair of pieces, carefully place them together as they will be sewn, and feed them into the machine one after the other.
3. Stop between each pair only long enough to pick up the next pair; don't cut thread between pairs (**Fig. 10**).

Fig. 10

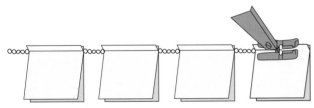

4. After all pieces are sewn, cut threads, press, and go on to the next step, chain piecing when possible.

Sewing Bias Seams

Care should be used in handling and stitching bias edges since they stretch easily. After sewing the seam, carefully press seam allowance to one side, making sure not to stretch fabric.

Sewing Across Seam Intersections

When sewing across the intersection of 2 seams, place pieces right sides together and match seams exactly, making sure seam allowances are pressed in opposite directions (**Fig. 11**).

Fig. 11

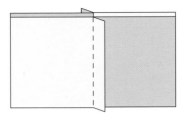

Trimming Seam Allowances

When sewing with triangle pieces, some seam allowances may extend beyond the edges of the sewn pieces. Trim away "dog ears" that extend beyond the edges of the sewn pieces (**Fig. 12**).

Fig. 12

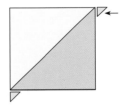

PRESSING

- When making pieced blocks, plan your pressing carefully.
- Use a steam iron set on "Cotton" for all pressing.
- Set the seams before pressing by placing the iron on the stitched seam line.
- Press seams as you sew them, normally to one side and toward the darker fabric or in the direction that will give the least bulk, taking care to prevent small folds along seamlines. Press the seams on the right side of the fabric.
- If you accidentally press the seam in the wrong direction, repress the seam closed then press again in the opposite direction.
- **All fringed seams must be pressed open.**

Annis Clapp

Annis Clapp's mother always believed that her daughter was a seamstress by nature. "She says that as a child I used to sit and watch her sew," Annis admits, "but I was too young to remember."

What Annis does remember are the handmade quilts she and her eight siblings used throughout their childhood on an Idaho strawberry farm. The bedspreads were a collaborative effort — her paternal grandmother pieced the tops, and her mother lovingly quilted them.

As she grew older, Annis' love for sewing and quilting grew as well. In the 1980's Annis sold her first quilt pattern to a local company. The following decade she still spent her spare time making and selling gift items at craft shows. Finally, in 2000, she entered a new season of life and started designing full time. She didn't really find her niche until she discovered rag quilting a year later. "I knew instantly that I had a winner," she says.

And like many quilters, Annis reveals that although she enjoys the work, her favorite part of quilting is seeing the finished product. "I like things that go together quickly … I like to see how it all comes together," she confesses.

Annis considers herself a self-taught seamstress — she gained much of her sewing and quilting knowledge through reading, asking questions, or trial and error. When she's not quilting or designing, Annis passes time with other needlecrafts such as crochet and needlepoint on plastic canvas. She also enjoys reading and designing floor plans for houses (she designed the house she and her husband built and have lived in for 26 years!).